by Iain Gray

Lang**Syne**

PUBLISHING

WRITING *to* REMEMBER

LangSyne

PUBLISHING

WRITING *to* REMEMBER

79 Main Street, Newtongrange,
Midlothian EH22 4NA
Tel: 0131 344 0414   Fax: 0845 075 6085
E-mail: info@lang-syne.co.uk
www.langsyneshop.co.uk

Design by Dorothy Meikle
Printed by Ricoh Print Scotland
© Lang Syne Publishers Ltd 2013

ISBN 978-1-85217-462-0

Blair

MOTTO:
I love the virtuous
(or) By virtue safe.

CREST:
A stag
(and)
A dove with wings expanded.

TERRITORY:
Ayrshire and Perthshire.

NAME variations include:
Blare
Blaire
Blayr
Bleher

*The spirit of the clan means
much to thousands of people*

Chapter one:

The origins of the clan system

by Rennie McOwan

The original Scottish clans of the Highlands and the great families of the Lowlands and Borders were gatherings of families, relatives, allies and neighbours for mutual protection against rivals or invaders.

Scotland experienced invasion from the Vikings, the Romans and English armies from the south. The Norman invasion of what is now England also had an influence on land-holding in Scotland. Some of these invaders stayed on and in time became 'Scottish'.

The word clan derives from the Gaelic language term 'clann', meaning children, and it was first used many centuries ago as communities were formed around tribal lands in glens and mountain fastnesses.

The format of clans changed over the centuries, but at its best the chief and his family held the land on behalf of all, like trustees, and the ordinary clansmen and women believed they had a blood relationship with the founder of their clan.

There were two way duties and obligations. An inadequate chief could be deposed and replaced by someone of greater ability.

Clan people had an immense pride in race. Their relationship with the chief was like adult children to a father and they had a real dignity.

The concept of clanship is very old and a more feudal notion of authority gradually crept in.

Pictland, for instance, was divided into seven principalities ruled by feudal leaders who were the strongest and most charismatic leaders of their particular groups.

By the sixth century the 'British' kingdoms of Strathclyde, Lothian and Celtic Dalriada (Argyll) had emerged and Scotland, as one nation, began to take shape in the time of King Kenneth MacAlpin.

Some chiefs claimed descent from ancient kings which may not have been accurate in every case.

By the twelfth and thirteenth centuries the clans and families were more strongly brought under the central control of Scottish monarchs.

Lands were awarded and administered more and more under royal favour, yet the power of the area clan chiefs was still very great.

The long wars to ensure Scotland's

independence against the expansionist ideas of English monarchs extended the influence of some clans and reduced the lands of others.

Those who supported Scotland's greatest king, Robert the Bruce, were awarded the territories of the families who had opposed his claim to the Scottish throne.

In the Scottish Borders country – the notorious Debatable Lands – the great families built up a ferocious reputation for providing warlike men accustomed to raiding into England and occasionally fighting one another.

Chiefs had the power to dispense justice and to confiscate lands and clan warfare produced a society where martial virtues – courage, hardiness, tenacity – were greatly admired.

Gradually the relationship between the clans and the Crown became strained as Scottish monarchs became more orientated to life in the Lowlands and, on occasion, towards England.

The Highland clans spoke a different language, Gaelic, whereas the language of Lowland Scotland and the court was Scots and in more modern times, English.

Highlanders dressed differently, had different

customs, and their wild mountain land sometimes seemed almost foreign to people living in the Lowlands.

It must be emphasised that Gaelic culture was very rich and story-telling, poetry, piping, the clarsach (harp) and other music all flourished and were greatly respected.

Highland culture was different from other parts of Scotland but it was not inferior or less sophisticated.

Central Government, whether in London or Edinburgh, sometimes saw the Gaelic clans as a challenge to their authority and some sent expeditions into the Highlands and west to crush the power of the Lords of the Isles.

Nevertheless, when the eighteenth century Jacobite Risings came along the cause of the Stuarts was mainly supported by Highland clans.

The word Jacobite comes from the Latin for James – Jacobus. The Jacobites wanted to restore the exiled Stuarts to the throne of Britain.

The monarchies of Scotland and England became one in 1603 when King James VI of Scotland (1st of England) gained the English throne after Queen Elizabeth died.

The Union of Parliaments of Scotland and England, the Treaty of Union, took place in 1707.

Some Highland clans, of course, and Lowland families opposed the Jacobites and supported the incoming Hanoverians.

After the Jacobite cause finally went down at Culloden in 1746 a kind of ethnic cleansing took place. The power of the chiefs was curtailed. Tartan and the pipes were banned in law.

Many emigrated, some because they wanted to, some because they were evicted by force. In addition, many Highlanders left for the cities of the south to seek work.

Many of the clan lands became home to sheep and deer shooting estates.

But the warlike traditions of the clans and the great Lowland and Border families lived on, with their descendants fighting bravely for freedom in two world wars.

Remember the men from whence you came, says the Gaelic proverb, and to that could be added the role of many heroic women.

The spirit of the clan, of having roots, whether Highland or Lowland, means much to thousands of people.

*Clan warfare produced a society where courage
and tenacity were greatly admired*

Chapter two:

In freedom's cause

A name that has been present in Scotland from earliest times, Blair and its popular spelling variants that include Blare and Blaire, is derived from the Gaelic blar, indicating a field, normally a field of battle, or an open plain.

It is through this that it lends its name to several locations in Scotland that include Blair Atholl, Blairduff, Blairgowrie and Blairmore.

Although now found in large numbers throughout Scotland in particular and the United Kingdom, the Republic of Ireland, North America, Australia and New Zealand in general, Ayrshire and Perthshire are recognised as being the earliest territorial homes of two separate Scottish families of the name.

It was in what is now East Ayrshire, near the village of Darvel, that the Blairs flourished for centuries as the Blairs of Blair, while they also prospered in Perthshire as the Blairs of Balthayock.

The barony of Blair in Ayrshire was granted in the early years of the twelfth century, while the

Barony of the Blairs of Balthayock, near Kinnoull, was granted during the same period.

Blair House in Ayrshire, also known as Blair Castle, survives to this day as the highly impressive venue for functions ranging from weddings to both corporate and private hospitality.

Set within 400 acres of gardens and parklands and now owned by Luke and Caroline Borthwick, who trace a descent from the original Blairs of Blair, the castle has played host over the centuries to iconic historical figures that include Mary, Queen of Scots.

In Perthshire, Balthayock Castle remained the seat of the Blairs of Balthayock for almost 500 years, and its still hauntingly beautiful ruins dominate the local landscape to this day.

It was as staunch defenders of Scotland's freedom and independence that proud bearers of the Blair name first stamped their mark on the bloody tapestry that is the nation's early history.

Knighted during the reign from 1249 to 1286 of Alexander III, Sir Bryce de Blare was one of 18 Scottish nobles who were treacherously killed in June of 1296 after an English army under the command of Edward I, known as 'the Hammer of the Scots', invaded the northern kingdom and seized control of key strategic points.

These included the west coast port of Ayr and its castle – and it was here that Sir Bryce and his fellow noblemen were lured under the impression they had been invited to take part in negotiations.

In what has become known as the shameful 'Barns of Ayr' incident, they were overpowered by the English garrison of the castle and unceremoniously hanged from the rafters of one of its barns.

In May of the following year, the great freedom fighter William Wallace raised the banner of revolt against the English occupation of his home-land after slaying Sir William Heselrig, Sheriff of Lanark, in revenge for the killing of his young wife, Marion.

Proving an expert in the tactics of guerrilla warfare, Wallace and his hardened band of freedom fighters inflicted stunning defeats on the English garrisons.

This culminated in the liberation of practically all of Scotland following the battle of Stirling Bridge, on September 11, 1297.

The forces of Wallace and his able commander Sir William Murray had earlier met up and prepared to face yet another mighty English invasion force that had been hurriedly despatched north by Edward.

Despite having a force of only thirty-six cavalry and 8,000 foot soldiers, compared to an army under the Earl of Surrey that boasted no less than 200 knights and 10,000 foot soldiers, the Scots held a strategic advantage that they exploited to the full.

Positioning their forces on the heights of the Abbey Craig, on the outskirts of Stirling, and where the imposing Wallace Monument now stands, Wallace and Murray waited patiently as Essex's force slowly made its way across a narrow wooden bridge that spanned the waters of the Forth.

As the bulk of the English army crossed onto the marshy ground at the foot of the Abbey Craig, the piercing blast of a hunting horn signalled a ferocious charge down the hillside of massed ranks of Scottish spearmen.

Trapped on the boggy ground, the English were incapable of putting up any effective resistance.

They were hacked to death in their hundreds, while many others drowned in the fast-flowing waters of the Forth in their heavy armour as they attempted to make their way back across the narrow bridge.

Defeated at the battle of Falkirk on July 22,

1298, after earlier being appointed Guardian of Scotland, Sir William Wallace was eventually betrayed and captured in August of 1305.

On the black day for Scotland of August 23 of that year, he was brutally executed in London on the orders of a vengeful Edward.

One important chronicler of the life and times of Wallace was his chaplain, John Blair, the Benedictine monk born near Fife.

As Wallace's chaplain, Blair was a first-hand observer of both the freedom fighter's defeats and victories – and his chronicle is thought to have provided the main source material for the bard Blind Harry's epic poem *Blind Harry's Wallace*, written about 172 years after the freedom fighter's execution.

Both the date of Blair's birth and death are not known with certainty, but what is known is that he died some years after Wallace at the Benedictine monastery in Dunfermline.

Bearers of the Blair name were also prominent, as the Wars of Independence continued, in their support of the warrior king Robert the Bruce.

Noted among these was Roger de Blare, a nephew of Sir Bryce de Blare, and who was knighted by Bruce for his part in the king's victory at the battle of Bannockburn, when a 20,000-strong English army under Edward II was defeated by a Scots army less than half this strength.

Ironically, it was through a misguided sense of chivalry that the battle occurred in the first place.

By midsummer of 1313 the mighty fortress of Stirling Castle was occupied by an English garrison under the command of Sir Philip Mowbray.

Bruce's brother, Edward, agreed to a pledge by Mowbray that if the castle was not relieved by battle by midsummer of the following year, then he would surrender.

This made battle inevitable, and by June 23 of 1314 the two armies faced one another at Bannockburn, in sight of the castle.

It was on this day that Bruce slew the English knight Sir Henry de Bohun in single combat, but the battle proper was not fought until the following day, shortly after the rise of the midsummer sun.

The English cavalry launched a desperate but futile charge on the densely packed ranks of Scottish spearmen known as schiltrons, and by the time the sun had sank slowly in the west the English army had been totally routed, with Edward himself only narrowly managing to make his escape from the carnage of the battlefield.

Scotland's independence had been secured, to the glory of Bruce and his loyal army and supporters such as Roger de Blare and at terrible cost to the English.

In the seventeenth century, bearers of the Blair name became embroiled in the bitter religious controversies of their time.

Born in 1593 in Irvine, Ayrshire, Robert Blair went through many trials, including excommunication for his Presbyterian views, before serving for a time as Moderator of the General Assembly of the Church of Scotland.

He was a supporter of the National Covenant – which renounced Catholic belief, pledged to uphold the Presbyterian religion, and called for free parliaments and assemblies.

Signed at Edinburgh's Greyfriars Church on February 28, 1638 by Scotland's nobles, barons, burgesses and ministers such as Blair, it was subscribed to the following day by hundreds of ordinary people.

Copies were made and dispatched around Scotland and signed by thousands more.

Those who adhered to the Covenant were

known as Covenanters, and many such as Blair, hounded by the merciless authorities, literally took to the hills of south and southwest Scotland to worship at what were known as open-air conventicles.

Elected Moderator of the General Assembly in 1646, he fell foul of the authorities following the Restoration of Charles II in 1660 – and it was then that he took to the hills for a time as a Covenanter; he died in 1666.

Chapter three:

Politics and the pen

In rather more peaceful times, one of the Covenanting Robert Blair's grandsons was his namesake, the Scottish poet Robert Blair, born in Edinburgh in 1699 and whose best known work is the blank verse poem *The Grave*, published three years before his death in 1746.

He was the father of the eminent Scottish advocate and judge Robert Blair, Lord Avontoun, who was born in Edinburgh in 1741.

Solicitor General for Scotland from 1789 to 1806 and Dean of the Faculty of Advocates from 1801 to 1808, he also served as Lord President of the Court of Session from 1808 until his death three years later.

Another distinguished bearer of the name was the Church of Scotland minister Hugh Blair, who came to the fore during the great flowering of creative talent known as the Scottish Enlightenment.

Born in 1718 in Edinburgh, the son of a merchant, before his death in 1800 he became noted as the author of a number of religious discourses and also for his *Lectures on Rhetoric and Belles Lettres* and *A*

Critical Dissertation on the Poems of Ossian, Son of Fingal.

Born in Banffshire in 1656, James Blair was the Scottish clergyman who, after being ordained as a minister in the Church of Scotland, was later ordained in the Church of England.

Appointed Commissary in the Virginia Colony in 1687, he later became instrumental in the foundation of what remains to this day the centre of educational excellence known as the College of William and Mary, in Williamsburg, Virginia; he died in 1743.

Williamsburg was also the birthplace in 1732 of John Blair, recognised as one of the Founding Fathers of the United States.

A delegate from Virginia to the Constitutional Convention, in September of 1789 he was appointed by George Washington to the Supreme Court of the United States; he died in 1800, while Blair Street, in Madison, Wisconsin, was later named in his honour.

A controversial figure to this day over his support of, and British participation in, former U.S. President George W. Bush's invasion of Afghanistan in 2001 and the invasion of Saddam Hussein's Iraq two years later, Tony Blair is the former Labour Party politician who served as Prime Minister of the United Kingdom from May of 1997 to June of 2007.

Born Anthony Charles Lynton Blair in Edinburgh in 1953, he went on after education at Fettes College, Edinburgh, and Oxford University, to become a lawyer before entering politics in 1983 as Member of Parliament (MP) for the English seat of Sedgefield West.

He was selected as leader of the Labour Party eleven years later, and in a landslide General Election victory in 1997 became the youngest British Prime Minister to hold the post since 1812 – while it was also under his leadership of the Labour Party that the term 'New Labour' was coined.

Despite criticism of his policy on Afghanistan and Iraq, he is recognised as having played a key role in the Northern Ireland peace process and for his successful interventions in war-torn Kosovo in 1999 and Sierra Leone in 2001.

A recipient of the U.S. Presidential Medal of Freedom in addition to a number of other honours, he has also held the post of Middle East Peace Envoy, while his autobiography, *A Journey*, was published in 2010.

The former Prime Minister's father, Leo

Blair, born in 1923 in Filey, Yorkshire, the son of travelling entertainers, is the retired lecturer in law who was raised by adoptive parents in the Govan area of Glasgow.

Tony Blair's brother, Sir William Blair, born in 1950, is the prominent lawyer who was appointed a British High Court judge in 2008.

Known also by her professional name of Cherie Booth, Cherie Blair is the lawyer who married Tony Blair in 1980.

Born in 1954 in Bury, Lancashire, a daughter of the actor Tony Booth and the actress Gale Howard, she is now patron of the charitable Cherie Blair Foundation and author of the 2008 autobiography *Speaking for Myself.*

A contemporary of Tony Blair during part of his tenure as Prime Minister, Ian Blair served as Commissioner of the Metropolitan Police, London, from 2005 to 2008.

Born in 1953 in Cheshire, the former police officer was appointed a life peer in the House of Lords in 2010 as Baron Blair of Boughton, in the County of Cheshire.

Combining both music and politics, Harold Blair was the Australian tenor and activist on behalf of

Aboriginal rights who was born in 1924 on the Cherbourg Aboriginal Reserve, Queensland.

It was after entering a radio talent show in 1945 that he was able to formally study music, including at the famed Julliard School, New York.

He was offered a three-year singing contract by the Australian Broadcasting Corporation in 1951, but tragedy struck when he lost his voice.

With his music career now seemingly at an end, he took on a number of other jobs, including working in a hardware store, before being appointed a teacher of music at the Conservatorium in Melbourne.

Also serving on the Aboriginal Arts Board as a passionate advocate of Aboriginal rights, he died in 1976 – after being appointed a member of the Order of Australia.

The Australian electoral division of Blair, in Queensland, was named in his honour in 1998.

Chapter four:

On the world stage

Bearers of the Blair name have flourished, and continue to flourish, through a colourfully diverse range of pursuits.

Beginning her career at the tender age of six as a child model, **Linda Blair** is the American actress best known for her disturbing role as the Satanically-possessed child, Regan, in the 1973 film *The Exorcist*, for which she received an Academy Award nomination and a Golden Globe Award.

Reprising her role in *Exorcist II*, she has also starred in other films that include the 1977 *Heretic* and the 1996 *Scream*, and, from 2012, *An Affair of the Heart*.

Born in 1959 in St Louis, Missouri, she was the recipient in 2008 of the Malaga Fantasy and Horror Film Festival Lifetime Achievement Award for her work in the horror genre.

Working in theatre, film and television, **Selma Blair** is the American actress born Selma Blair Beitner in Southfield, Michigan, in 1972.

In addition to having played the role of Kim

in the American version of the television sitcom *Kath and Kim*, she has also appeared in films that include the 1996 *The Broccoli Theory*, the 2001 *Legally Blonde*, and, from 2012, *Columbas Circle*.

Best known for her role as Carmella Cammeniti from 2003 to 2009 on the Australian television soap *Neighbours*, **Natalie Blair** is the actress born in 1984 in Brisbane.

Winner in 2005 of the Most Popular New Female Talent Award at the annual Australian Logie Awards, she won a Gold Logie Award in 2008 for Most Popular Personality on Australian Television.

Born Henry Blair Ogus in Montreal, Canada, in 1931, **Lionel Blair** is the multi-talented choreographer, tap dancer and television presenter who settled in Britain with his family only a year after his birth.

Along with his older sister, Joyce, he gave his first public performance – tap dancing and singing – in London Underground air raid shelters during the Second World War.

Attending the Royal Shakespeare Theatre in Stratford for a time, followed by performances in London's West End, he gave up acting in preference to dancing in 1947.

Appearing with his dance troupe throughout

the 1960s in a number of British television variety programmes, he also made an appearance in the Beatles film, *A Hard Day's Night*.

As a choreographer, he was involved in films that include the 1960 *The Jazz Boat*, and, nine years later, *The Magic Christian*, while also appearing on television shows such as *Give Us a Clue* and presenting *Name that Tune*.

His sister, Joyce, born in 1932, also took to the stage as a dancer and actress, appearing in television shows that included *The Morecambe and Wise Show*, and also in her brother's-choreographed film *The Jazz Boat*.

The mother of British actress Deborah Sheridan-Taylor, she died in 2006.

In the creative world of film animation, **Preston Blair**, born in 1908 in Redlands, California, and who died in 2005, was the American character animator noted for his work at Walt Disney Productions and the animation department of MGM.

He was a brother of the artist **Lee Blair**, born in 1911 and who died in 1993. He, in turn, was the husband of the artist and animator **Mary Blair**.

Born Mary McAlester in 1911 in Oklahoma,

she drew art work for Disney films that include *Alice in Wonderland*, *Peter Pan* and *Cinderella*.

The artist, who died in 1978, was later honoured as a Disney Legend.

Bearers of the Blair name have also gained distinction on the bloody field of battle.

Born in 1834, **Robert Blair** was a Scottish recipient of the Victoria Cross (VC), the highest award for gallantry in the face of enemy action for British and Commonwealth forces.

He had been a lieutenant in the 2nd Dragoon Guards, attached to the 9th Lancers (Queen's Royals) during the Indian Mutiny, when, in September of 1857 at Bolandshahr, he was ordered to take a party of men to recover an abandoned ammunition wagon.

He successfully carried out the mission, with no loss of his own men, although he was seriously wounded; later promoted to the rank of captain, he died in India nearly two years later from smallpox.

His VC is now on display at the Queen's Dragoon Guards Regimental Museum in Cardiff, Wales.

He was a cousin of **General James Blair**, who was also a recipient of the VC for his actions during the Indian Mutiny.

Born in what was then British India in 1828, he had been a captain in the 2nd Bombay Light Cavalry when, in August of 1857, he single-handedly captured seven armed mutineers, despite being wounded, while just over two months later he managed to fight his way out of a band of mutineers who had surrounded him.

Later promoted to the rank of general, he died in 1905 at his home in Melrose, in the Scottish Borders.

Bearers of the Blair name have also excelled in the highly competitive world of sport.

In rugby, **Mike Blair**, born in 1981 in Edinburgh, is the Scottish rugby union scrum-half who made his debut for the national team in 2002, and who has since captained it.

He is an older brother of rugby union player **David Blair**, born in 1985, who has played for Edinburgh Gunners.

In European football, **Jimmy Blair**, born in 1888 in Glenboig, Lanarkshire, and who died in 1964, was the defender who, in addition to playing for teams that include Sheffield Wednesday and Cardiff City, earned eight caps playing for Scotland between 1920 and 1924.

His son, also **Jimmy Blair**, born in 1918 in Whiteinch, Glasgow, and who died in 1983, was the forward who played for Scotland in 1946, while another son, **Doug Blair**, born in 1921, is the former inside forward who played for teams that include Blackpool and Hereford United.

In addition to earning nine caps for Scotland between 1929 and 1933, **Danny Blair** was the Scottish footballer, born in Parkhead, Glasgow, in 1905, who also played for a time in North America with teams that included Toronto's Davenport Albion and the Providence Clamdiggers of the American Soccer League; he died in 1985.

In speed-skating, **Bonnie Blair** is the retired American speed-skater who was born in 1964 in Cornwall, New York.

She is recognised as one of the top skaters of all time and one of the most decorated athletes in Winter Olympics history – winning five gold medals and one bronze through the 500-metre and 1,000-metre events.

Elected to the United States Olympic Hall of fame in 2004, she is married to fellow Olympic speed-skater Dave Cruikshank.

From skating to badminton, **Robert Blair** is

the Scottish player who was born in Edinburgh in 1981 and whose wins include a silver medal in Men's Doubles at the 2006 World Championships.

On the cricket pitch, **Bob Blair**, born in 1932, is the former New Zealand cricketer who played in 19 Test Matches for his country.

In the creative world of the written word, Eric Blair was the essayist, journalist and novelist better known by his pen-name of **George Orwell**.

Born in 1903 in what was then British India, where his father worked in the Civil Service, but later brought up in Henley-on-Thames, near London, he is considered one of the twentieth century's greatest writers.

His experience of fighting on the side of the Republicans during the Spanish Civil War resulted in his 1938 *Homage to Catalonia*, while he is also renowned for *Animal Farm*, published in 1945, and *Nineteen Eighty-Four*, published four years later.

Other major works include *Burmese Days*, *Down and Out in Paris and London*, *The Road to Wigan Pier*, *Coming up for Air* and *Keep the Aspidistra Flying*.

Dogged by ill-health throughout his life, particularly after being wounded in the throat by a sniper's bullet while fighting in Spain, he died in 1950.

A best-selling author of romantic fiction, **Emma Blair** was not quite all 'she' seemed.

The writer, in fact, was a former Scottish actor by the name of **Iain Blair**, born in Glasgow in 1942 and who died in 2011.

Following roles in a number of British television dramas that included *The Sweeney, Juliet Bravo* and the sitcom *Citizen Smith*, he turned his talents to romantic fiction – suggesting to his publisher that his books would sell better if readers thought they had been penned by a woman.

It was therefore under the nom-de-plume of Emma Blair that his first romantic novel, *Where No Man Cries*, was published, and it was not until 1998, that Emma Blair's true identity was officially revealed by his publishers to a wider public when his *Flower of Scotland* was nominated for Romantic Novel of the Year.

His widow, the author and television producer Jane Blanchard, said: "Emma Blair was not the quiet, retiring type, but a 6ft. 3ins. Glaswegian called Iain Blair, who enjoyed a pint and a smoke."

One particularly enterprising bearer of the

Blair name was **John Insley Blair**, the American entrepreneur recognised as having been one of the nineteenth century's wealthiest men.

Born in 1802 in Foul Rift, near Belvidere, New Jersey, to parents who had settled there from Scotland, an early sign of his entrepreneurial ambition manifested itself at the age of ten, when he told his parents: "I have seven brothers and three sisters. That's enough in the family to be educated – I am going to get rich!"

He began earning money by trapping and selling rabbits and muskrats, before working in a store owned by a cousin.

By the age of 17, he had founded another store with his cousin and by 1830 owned five stores in his own right.

His fortunes flourished to the extent that he eventually became president of no less than 16 railroad companies.

He died in 1899, having amassed a personal fortune estimated at $70m, while both Princeton University, New Jersey, and Grinnell College, Iowa, were only two of the many beneficiaries of his philanthropy.